YORK NOTES

C000000261

THE SIGN OF THE FOUR

AQA PRACTICE TESTS WITH ANSWERS

JO HEATHCOTE

The right of Jo Heathcote to be identified as the Author of this Work
has been asserted by her in accordance with the Copyright,
Designs and Patents Act 1988

YORK PRESS
322 Old Brompton Road, London SW5 9JH

PEARSON EDUCATION LIMITED
Edinburgh Gate, Harlow,
Essex CM20 2JE, United Kingdom
Associated companies, branches and representatives throughout the world

First published 2018

10 9 8 7 6 5 4 3 2 1

ISBN 978–1–2922–3685–8

Phototypeset by Swales and Willis Ltd
Printed in Slovakia

Photo credits: LStockStudio/Shutterstock for page 6 bottom / michaeljung/Shutterstock for
page 49 bottom / Monkey Business Images / Shutterstock for page 50 bottom

CONTENTS

PART ONE: INTRODUCTION

How to use these practice tests

This book contains seven GCSE English Literature exam-style practice tests for *The Sign of the Four*. All the York Notes tests have been modelled on the ones that you will sit in your AQA GCSE 9–1 English Literature exam.

There are lots of ways these tests can support your study and revision for your AQA English Literature exam on *The Sign of the Four*. There is no 'right' way – choose the one (or ones) that suits your learning style best:

1 Alongside the York Notes Study Guide for *The Sign of the Four*

Do you have the York Notes Study Guide for *The Sign of the Four*?

These tests will allow you to try out all the skills and techniques outlined in the Study Guide. So you could:

- choose a question from this book
- read the sections of the Study Guide relevant to the question, i.e. Plot and Action; Characters; Themes, Contexts and Setting; Structure, Form and Language
- use the Progress Booster exam section of the Study Guide to remind yourself of key exam techniques
- complete the question.

2 As a stand-alone revision programme

Do you know the text inside out and have you already mastered the skills needed for your exam?

If so, you can keep your skills fresh by answering one or two questions from this book each day or week in the lead-up to the exam. You could make a revision diary and allocate particular questions to particular times.

3 As a form of mock exam

Would you like to test yourself under exam conditions?

You could put aside part of a day to work on a practice test in a quiet room. Set a stopwatch so that you can experience what it will be like in your real exam. If some of your friends have copies of this book then several of you could all do this together and discuss your answers afterwards.

Or, you could try working through Part Two of this book slowly, question by question, over a number of days as part of your revision, and save the further questions in Part Three to use as a mock test.

How to use the answer sections

This book contains a mixture of annotated sample answers and short (indicative content) answers that will help you to:

- identify the difference between Mid, Good and Very High Level work

- understand how the Assessment Objectives are applied

- grade your own answers by comparing them with the samples provided.

The answers can also give you additional ideas for your responses and help you to aim high.

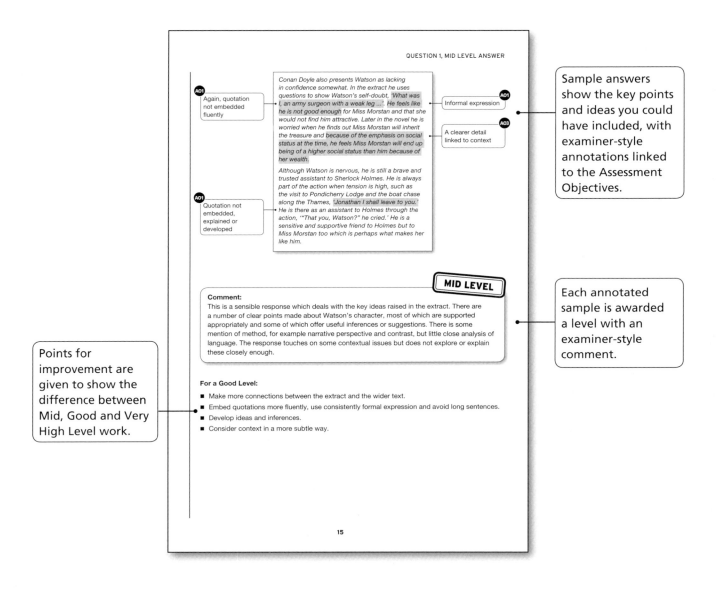

QUESTION 1, MID LEVEL ANSWER

A01 Again, quotation not embedded fluently

Conan Doyle also presents Watson as lacking in confidence somewhat. In the extract he uses questions to show Watson's self-doubt, 'What was I, an army surgeon with a weak leg ...'. He feels like he is not good enough for Miss Morstan and that she would not find him attractive. Later in the novel he is worried when he finds out Miss Morstan will inherit the treasure and because of the emphasis on social status at the time, he feels Miss Morstan will end up being of a higher social status than him because of her wealth.

A01 Informal expression

A03 A clearer detail linked to context

A01 Quotation not embedded, explained or developed

Although Watson is nervous, he is still a brave and trusted assistant to Sherlock Holmes. He is always part of the action when tension is high, such as the visit to Pondicherry Lodge and the boat chase along the Thames, 'Jonathan I shall leave to you.' He is there as an assistant to Holmes through the action, '"That you, Watson?" he cried.' He is a sensitive and supportive friend to Holmes but to Miss Morstan too which is perhaps what makes her like him.

MID LEVEL

Comment:
This is a sensible response which deals with the key ideas raised in the extract. There are a number of clear points made about Watson's character, most of which are supported appropriately and some of which offer useful inferences or suggestions. There is some mention of method, for example narrative perspective and contrast, but little close analysis of language. The response touches on some contextual issues but does not explore or explain these closely enough.

For a Good Level:
- Make more connections between the extract and the wider text.
- Embed quotations more fluently, use consistently formal expression and avoid long sentences.
- Develop ideas and inferences.
- Consider context in a more subtle way.

15

Sample answers show the key points and ideas you could have included, with examiner-style annotations linked to the Assessment Objectives.

Each annotated sample is awarded a level with an examiner-style comment.

Points for improvement are given to show the difference between Mid, Good and Very High Level work.

Assessment Objectives and weightings

Your work on *The Sign of the Four* will be examined through the three Assessment Objectives (AOs) listed below:

AO1	Read, understand and respond to texts. You should be able to: • maintain a critical style and develop an informed personal response • use textual references, including quotations, to support and illustrate interpretations.
AO2	Analyse the language, form and structure used by a writer to create meanings and effects, using relevant subject terminology where appropriate.
AO3	Show understanding of the relationships between texts and the contexts in which they were written.

The marks allocated by AQA for each Assessment Objective are as follows:

AO1	12 marks
AO2	12 marks
AO3	6 marks
Total (per question)	30 marks

Knowing the number of marks allowed for each AO is important, as this will help you to achieve the right balance of key skills and techniques in your answer.

Mark scheme

The annotated sample answers that follow Questions 1 to 4 in this book have been given a Level based on the mark schemes below.*

Lower Level

AO1	You give some relevant responses to the set task and use some suitable references.
AO2	You identify some of the writer's methods but do not always comment effectively on them.
AO3	You show some awareness of contextual factors but find it difficult to link them to the text.

Mid Level

AO1	You give a clear response and select suitable references and quotations.
AO2	You make clear references to the writer's methods to support your points.
AO3	You make clear links between some aspects of context and the text.

Turn to page 8 for the mark schemes for Good to High and Very High Levels.

* These are 'student-friendly' mark schemes and are a guide only.

Good to High Level

AO1	You demonstrate very effective understanding of the task and text, and choose references and quotations carefully.
AO2	You analyse carefully and comment consistently well on the writer's methods, interpreting ideas.
AO3	You make very effective links between context and the text.

Very High Level

AO1	You have a broad, conceptualised idea of the text, and make well-judged and wide-ranging use of references and quotations.
AO2	You are analytical and explore the text precisely and convincingly. You comment in finely tuned detail on the writer's use of language, form and structure.
AO3	You write convincingly and relevantly about a wide range of contextual factors.

Now you know what you're aiming for, you can begin the practice tests.

Turn to page 10 for Question 1.*

The extracts from The Sign of the Four used in these Practice Tests are taken from the Collins Classic edition, 2015.

PART TWO: YORK NOTES PRACTICE TESTS WITH ANNOTATED SAMPLE ANSWERS

Question 1

Read the following extract from Chapter 2 of *The Sign of the Four* (page 16).

In this extract, Dr Watson reflects on his first meeting with Miss Morstan.

> I sat in the window with the volume in my hand, but my
> thoughts were far from the daring speculations of the writer. My
> mind ran upon our late visitor, – her smiles, the deep rich tones
> of her voice, the strange mystery which overhung her life. If she
> 5 were seventeen at the time of her father's disappearance she
> must be seven-and-twenty now, – a sweet age, when youth
> has lost its self-conscious and become a little sobered by
> experience. So I sat and mused, until such dangerous thoughts
> came into my head that I hurried away to my desk and plunged
> 10 furiously into the latest treatise upon pathology. What was I, an
> army surgeon with a weak leg and a weaker banking-account,
> that I should dare to think of such things? She was a unit, a
> factor, – nothing more. If my future were black, it was better
> surely to face it like a man than to attempt to brighten it by mere
> 15 will-o'-the-wisps of the imagination.

Starting with this extract, explore how Conan Doyle presents the character of Dr Watson.

Write about:

■ how Conan Doyle presents Dr Watson in this extract
■ how Conan Doyle presents Dr Watson in the novel as a whole.

[30 marks]

Annotated sample answers

Now, read the three sample answers that follow and, based on what you have read, try to allocate a level to your own work. Which of the three responses is your answer closest to? Don't be discouraged if your work doesn't seem as strong as some of the responses here – the point is to use these samples to learn about what is needed and then put it into practice in your own work. Conversely, you may have mentioned relevant ideas or points that don't appear in these responses; if this is the case, give yourself a pat on the back – it shows you are considering lots of good ideas.

Sample answer A

AO2
Considers a method the writer uses, with support, but quotation could be more fluently embedded

Dr Watson is Sherlock Holmes's assistant. He is an interesting character. He is also the narrator of the novel and the story is told through his eyes because he says, 'I sat in the window ...'. In the extract we see that Watson is thinking back over the meeting with Miss Morstan. He is worried about her and thinks she is involved in a 'strange mystery'. This helps us to think about the mystery ahead and how it may be solved.

AO2
Useful structural point, simply put

Watson is a close friend of Holmes and knows all of his cases. He is a writer as well as a doctor and has written up some of Holmes's cases as stories. He seems to be more imaginative than some of the other men in the novel because Conan Doyle uses him as a contrast to Holmes who is very methodical and rational, '"My dear Watson, try a little analysis yourself," said he' with a touch of impatience and we get the impression Watson is a bit more of a dreamer. In the extract he is thinking about Miss Morstan, not just because of the mystery but because he also finds her attractive. He comments on 'her smiles, the deep rich tones of her voice' and this implies he has paid attention to Miss Morstan. This is different from Holmes's view of her as a client, 'a unit, a factor'. However, he describes his reaction to her using the phrase 'dangerous thoughts' and knows that he should not be thinking of her in this way telling us something about the way middle-class men felt they should behave to middle-class women at the time.

AO1
Shows knowledge about Watson's character and makes a useful inference

AO2
Another method is touched on and supported, but the sentence could be shorter

AO2
Develops the idea of contrast and makes a link to the language choices in the extract

AO3
Touches on a point of context but does not explore or develop it; another long sentence

As well as caring about Miss Morstan and the case, Watson is very sensitive. He does sometimes feel hurt by how blunt Holmes can be, for example when Holmes is insensitive about Watson's brother's death, 'I sprang from my chair and limped impatiently about the room with considerable bitterness in my heart' and when Watson announces his engagement to Miss Morstan at the end, 'I was a little hurt'.

AO1
Shows a wider knowledge of the text linked to a point about Watson's character; quotation could be embedded more fluently

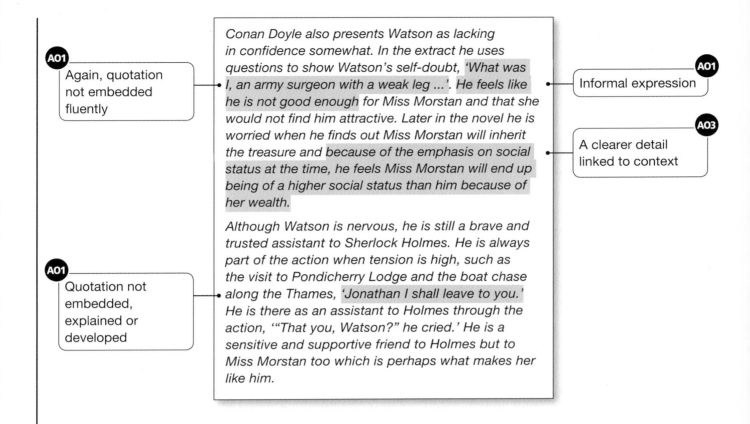

AO1 — Again, quotation not embedded fluently

AO1 — Quotation not embedded, explained or developed

> Conan Doyle also presents Watson as lacking in confidence somewhat. In the extract he uses questions to show Watson's self-doubt, 'What was I, an army surgeon with a weak leg ...'. He feels like he is not good enough for Miss Morstan and that she would not find him attractive. Later in the novel he is worried when he finds out Miss Morstan will inherit the treasure and because of the emphasis on social status at the time, he feels Miss Morstan will end up being of a higher social status than him because of her wealth.
>
> Although Watson is nervous, he is still a brave and trusted assistant to Sherlock Holmes. He is always part of the action when tension is high, such as the visit to Pondicherry Lodge and the boat chase along the Thames, 'Jonathan I shall leave to you.' He is there as an assistant to Holmes through the action, '"That you, Watson?" he cried.' He is a sensitive and supportive friend to Holmes but to Miss Morstan too which is perhaps what makes her like him.

AO1 — Informal expression

AO3 — A clearer detail linked to context

MID LEVEL

Comment:

This is a sensible response which deals with the key ideas raised in the extract. There are a number of clear points made about Watson's character, most of which are supported appropriately and some of which offer useful inferences or suggestions. There is some mention of method, for example narrative perspective and contrast, but little close analysis of language. The response touches on some contextual issues but does not explore or explain these closely enough.

For a Good Level:

- Make more connections between the extract and the wider text.
- Embed quotations more fluently, use consistently formal expression and avoid long sentences.
- Develop ideas and inferences.
- Consider context in a more subtle way.

Sample answer B

AO2

Begins by establishing Watson's role as part of the structure of the novel

AO1

Uses some effective textual details to explore the language choices connected to Watson as well as establishing the key idea of the extract

AO3

A clearly expressed idea linked to a contextual aspect of the novel, but could be developed further

AO1

An interesting and perceptive idea

Conan Doyle presents us with an interesting character in Dr Watson, in that he is not just a character and part of the action, but he is also the framework narrator for the novel and he holds together all of the storytelling that takes place.

In this extract we are told his thoughts and reflections on the meeting with Miss Morstan when he tells us, 'My mind ran upon our late visitor'. Watson reveals his human and more romantic side compared with the 'automaton' Holmes, in that he clearly finds Miss Morstan very attractive and refers to her with softened romantic language, such as 'a sweet age', 'her self-control was perfect', 'the sweet face of Mary Morstan looking down upon me.' However, his sense of doing right means that he dismisses these thoughts as 'dangerous' suggesting that he has a strong moral code and is highly respectful of women.

In addition, he clearly has doubts about himself when he questions how Miss Morstan could ever be interested in an 'army surgeon with a weak leg'. Watson sees himself as not being worthy of her. This is emphasised even more later on in the novel when it seems likely that Miss Morstan will become very wealthy through the inheritance of the Agra treasure. Watson says, 'The Agra treasure intervened like an impassable barrier between us' – he worries she will be of a higher social status than him as a result.

Watson's feelings of doubt could stem from his relationship with Holmes who Watson believes is something of a 'genius' in comparison to himself. Holmes's reputation and 'mind that rebels against stagnation' could be an intimidating thing for Watson as Holmes does, on occasion, behave very insensitively towards him. Even at the end of the novel after all the support Watson has given, Holmes tells Watson, 'I really cannot congratulate you' on the news of his engagement. However, it is clear that Holmes values Watson's company, loyalty and friendship and he accompanies Holmes though all of the major action in the novel.

Watson is used as a device by Conan Doyle to reflect on the action, asking 'How, for example, could you describe with such confidence the wooden-legged man?' In this way Watson acts on our behalf, asking the questions of Holmes we want to ask in order to keep track of the mystery.

AO1

A useful and relevant inference made from a textual detail, fluently embedded

AO1

This could be explored further

AO2

A clearly expressed consideration of one of the writer's methods

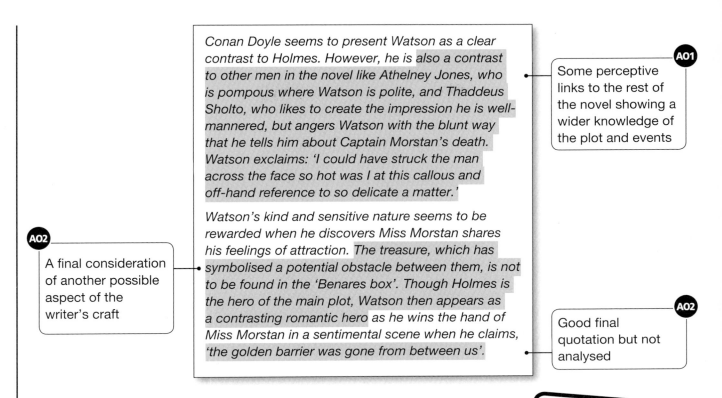

AO1

Some perceptive links to the rest of the novel showing a wider knowledge of the plot and events

Conan Doyle seems to present Watson as a clear contrast to Holmes. However, he is also a contrast to other men in the novel like Athelney Jones, who is pompous where Watson is polite, and Thaddeus Sholto, who likes to create the impression he is well-mannered, but angers Watson with the blunt way that he tells him about Captain Morstan's death. Watson exclaims: 'I could have struck the man across the face so hot was I at this callous and off-hand reference to so delicate a matter.'

AO2

A final consideration of another possible aspect of the writer's craft

Watson's kind and sensitive nature seems to be rewarded when he discovers Miss Morstan shares his feelings of attraction. The treasure, which has symbolised a potential obstacle between them, is not to be found in the 'Benares box'. Though Holmes is the hero of the main plot, Watson then appears as a contrasting romantic hero as he wins the hand of Miss Morstan in a sentimental scene when he claims, 'the golden barrier was gone from between us'.

AO2

Good final quotation but not analysed

GOOD LEVEL

Comment:

This is a generally confident response, which shows a good knowledge of the novel and of Watson's role within it. There is a wide range of supporting material drawn not just from the extract but from the whole text. Many of the textual details have thoughtful comments and inferences drawn from them and there is an attempt to embed quotations into the response. There is an emphasis on the craft of the writer and there is some clear consideration of how Conan Doyle is utilising Watson as a device to drive the action forward. Some subtle contextual details are integrated into the response.

For a High Level:

- Develop a more mature style which considers other possible interpretations and inferences.
- Make more effective use of quotations to develop inferences.
- Explore the craft of the writer with more precision and fluency to pinpoint the effects in a more developed way.

Sample answer C

AO1 Uses the text in a well-chosen way to open the essay

AO2 Well-chosen textual references to support the point

AO1 A developed interpretation of character with an apt textual detail

AO1 An interesting link between ideas

AO2 Sophisticated use of subject terminology

AO3 A subtle contextual link

'In God's name, what does it all mean?' asks Watson. His question could also be that of the reader as, in this novel, Watson acts not only as a central character but one whose first-person perspective illuminates the mystery for us through his conversations with Holmes. In addition, Watson acts as a framework narrator who holds together the various stories woven into the plot: those of Thaddeus Sholto's 'extraordinary narrative', Jonathan Small's 'remarkable account' and Miss Morstan's 'strange mystery'. Every aspect of the plot is filtered through his consciousness and as a result we are encouraged to trust his judgements. As modern readers, however, we are compelled to question his judgements at times: Watson's views represent the attitudes of the British educated middle classes of the time, and can be disturbing; for example, Watson's perceptions of Tonga as a 'savage distorted creature'.

Despite this, Watson often shows a much more sensitive side and provides a contrast to the lack of sensitivity displayed by other characters, notably Holmes. The detective's deeply logical mind can at times allow him to be hurtful and dismissive of Watson's gentler and more imaginative qualities, leaving Watson with 'considerable bitterness'. Watson, however, is well aware of Holmes's emotional shortcomings and shares his frustrations with us, 'irritated by the egotism' of his friend. This allows Conan Doyle to present Watson as a more sympathetic character and a more reliable narrator.

At the same time, Watson is loyal and solicitous of Holmes and this aspect of his character is also seen in his developing relationship with Miss Morstan. This is most notable at Pondicherry Lodge, where Conan Doyle contrasts the horror of Bartholomew's murder with references to 'love', 'affection' and 'peace' as Watson and Miss Morstan stand 'hand in hand, like two children'. This is a powerful image which prepares us for their romantic union.

It is following the initial meeting with Miss Morstan that Watson shows his reflective qualities. We witness his internal monologue as he comes to terms with the fact that he finds Holmes's new client highly attractive. He comments on her physical attributes, 'her smiles', 'the deep rich tones of her voice', which demonstrates that he is as keenly observant as Holmes but in a much less detached and dispassionate way.

A keen sense of propriety leads Watson to dismiss these 'dangerous thoughts' but we see how they are rekindled with every future meeting with Miss Morstan, for example in the initial cab ride through London

AO2 Some detailed consideration of two key methods, confidently opening the response

AO3 A well-integrated contextual link

AO2 Excellent structural inference and personal interpretation

AO2 Again, well-chosen references from the text are used to develop and support the idea; use of apt terminology

AO1 A perceptive and interesting idea

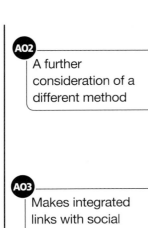

A02 A further consideration of a different method

A03 Makes integrated links with social context

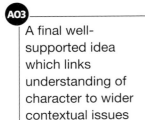

A03 A final well-supported idea which links understanding of character to wider contextual issues

when he notes her 'self-control was perfect', and at Thaddeus Sholto's house. Here Watson's hyperbole is almost humorous when he feels he could have 'struck the man across the face' for his lack of sensitivity in revealing the news of Captain Morstan's death.

Whilst being considerate of others, Watson is also self-deprecating and anxious about his own status. This is shown when he asks, 'What was I, an army soldier with a weak leg …?', revealing his self-doubt as to his worthiness to be a partner to Miss Morstan. Watson also faces anxieties about how the treasure would elevate Miss Morstan from a 'needy governess to the richest heiress in England'. This is presented as an obstacle to a potential courtship, showing us how deeply entrenched ideas of class and status may have affected love relationships at the time.

Watson is used by Conan Doyle in many ways therefore: as a contrast to the brutality of the main plot, the dynamism of Holmes's thought processes and the heavy handed pomposity of Athelney Jones. Watson is also the romantic hero of the gentler sub-plot, which symbolises a restoration to order following the chaos of the main action and its dangerous links to colonised lands and 'savagery'. The romanticised vision of England is one that Watson clings to during the 'wild, dark business which had absorbed us', again revealing more of those conservative British values of the time, which are so evident elsewhere in the novel.

A02 Another strong and useful observation on method

VERY HIGH LEVEL

Comment:
This response shows a wide-ranging knowledge of the text and selects extremely apt quotations, which are embedded skilfully within the response. The ideas are mature and complex. Conan Doyle's methods and techniques are explored in a knowledgeable way and are again supported with apt and well-judged textual details. The response makes subtle and perceptive use of contextual ideas which link to the main points about Watson's character and lead to a confident response.

Question 2

Read the following extract from Chapter 8 of *The Sign of the Four* (pages 67–8).

In this extract, Sherlock Holmes and Watson arrive at Mordecai Smith's boatyard and Holmes speaks to Smith's son and wife.

'Dear little chap!' said Holmes, strategically. 'What a rosy-cheeked young rascal! Now, Jack, is there anything you would like?'

The youth pondered for a moment. 'I'd like a shillin'', said he.

'Nothing you would like better?'

5   'I'd like two shillin' better,' the prodigy answered, after some thought.

'Here you are, then! Catch! – A fine child, Mrs. Smith!'

'Lor' bless you, sir, he is that, and forward. He gets a'most too much for me to manage, 'specially when my man is away days at a time.'

'Away, is he?' said Holmes, in a disappointed voice. 'I am sorry for that, for I wanted to
10   speak to Mr. Smith.'

'He's been away since yesterday mornin', sir, and, truth to tell, I am beginnin' to feel frightened about him. But if it was about a boat, sir, maybe I could serve as well.'

'I wanted to hire his steam launch.'

'Why, bless you, sir, it is in the steam launch that he has gone. That's what puzzles me;
15   for I know there ain't more coals in her than would take her to about Woolwich and back. If he'd been away in the barge I'd ha' thought nothin'; for many a time a job has taken him as far as Gravesend, and then if there was much doin' there he might ha' stayed over. But what good is a steam launch without coals?'

'He might have bought some at a wharf down the river.'

20   'He might, sir, but it weren't his way. Many a time I've heard him call out at the prices they charge for a few odd bags. Besides, I don't like that wooden-legged man, wi' his ugly face and outlandish talk. What did he want always knockin' about here for?'

'A wooden-legged man?' said Holmes, with bland surprise.

'Yes, sir, a brown, monkey-faced chap that's called more'n once for my old man. It was
25   him that roused him up yesternight, and, what's more, my man knew he was comin', for he had steam up in the launch. I tell you straight, sir, I don't feel easy in my mind about it.'

Starting with this extract, explore how Conan Doyle presents issues of class and status.

Write about:

- how Conan Doyle presents issues of class and status in this extract
- how Conan Doyle presents issues of class and status in the novel as a whole.

[30 marks]

Annotated sample answers

Now, read the three sample answers that follow and, based on what you have read, try to allocate a level to your own work. Which of the three responses is your answer closest to? Don't be discouraged if your work doesn't seem as strong as some of the responses here – the point is to use these samples to learn about what is needed and then put it into practice in your own work. Conversely, you may have mentioned relevant ideas or points that don't appear in these responses; if this is the case, give yourself a pat on the back – it shows you are considering lots of good ideas.

Sample answer A

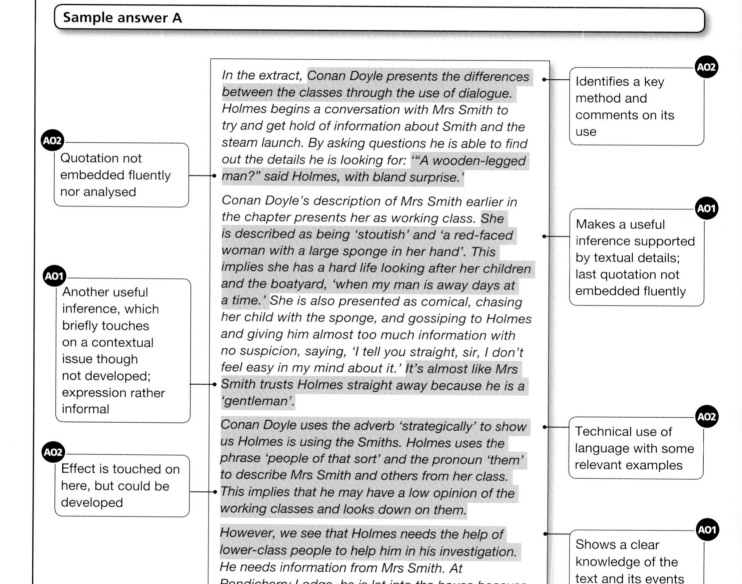

AO2 Quotation not embedded fluently nor analysed

In the extract, Conan Doyle presents the differences between the classes through the use of dialogue. Holmes begins a conversation with Mrs Smith to try and get hold of information about Smith and the steam launch. By asking questions he is able to find out the details he is looking for: '"A wooden-legged man?" said Holmes, with bland surprise.'

AO2 Identifies a key method and comments on its use

Conan Doyle's description of Mrs Smith earlier in the chapter presents her as working class. She is described as being 'stoutish' and 'a red-faced woman with a large sponge in her hand'. This implies she has a hard life looking after her children and the boatyard, 'when my man is away days at a time.' She is also presented as comical, chasing her child with the sponge, and gossiping to Holmes and giving him almost too much information with no suspicion, saying, 'I tell you straight, sir, I don't feel easy in my mind about it.' It's almost like Mrs Smith trusts Holmes straight away because he is a 'gentleman'.

AO1 Another useful inference, which briefly touches on a contextual issue though not developed; expression rather informal

AO1 Makes a useful inference supported by textual details; last quotation not embedded fluently

AO2 Effect is touched on here, but could be developed

Conan Doyle uses the adverb 'strategically' to show us Holmes is using the Smiths. Holmes uses the phrase 'people of that sort' and the pronoun 'them' to describe Mrs Smith and others from her class. This implies that he may have a low opinion of the working classes and looks down on them.

AO2 Technical use of language with some relevant examples

AO3 A useful contextual observation based on evidence of language used

However, we see that Holmes needs the help of lower-class people to help him in his investigation. He needs information from Mrs Smith. At Pondicherry Lodge, he is let into the house because he had wrestled McMurdo the prizefighter, who is guarding the place. He is also well known by Mr Sherman who tells Watson, 'A friend of Mr Sherlock is always welcome.' People from the working classes all seem to have much more respect for the upper classes than the upper classes have for them. Mrs Smith, Mr Sherman and McMurdo all call Holmes and Watson 'Sir'.

AO1 Shows a clear knowledge of the text and its events

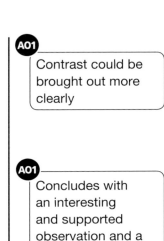

AO1

Contrast could be brought out more clearly

AO1

Concludes with an interesting and supported observation and a thoughtful inference

In another example, Holmes describes the workers as 'Dirty looking rascals' later in the novel when they are on the Thames. This implies the people are trouble-makers and not people who have worked hard all day. It seems to show that the upper classes do not have respect for people of a lower class.

However, we see that some of the lower-class characters have their own ranking system. Mrs Smith sees Jonathan Small as not being respectable and calls him 'a brown, monkey-faced chap'. Her suspicions are right though as he was a convict and ends up back in custody at the end of the novel. It seems that society at the time was very structured and that your social status and class can affect where you end up in life.

AO3

Repeats idea about social context, which could be developed

MID LEVEL

Comment:

This is a generally sensible response, which explains a number of ideas clearly in relation to the task. The answer uses several textual references and supporting quotations, though these are not always embedded and used skilfully. Some of the writer's methods are identified, but these tend to be connected with language use only and there is room for some further development here. There are also some useful observations about social context, though again these could be explored in more detail.

For a Good Level:

- Make more effective use of quotations.
- Consider other methods Conan Doyle uses in the novel.
- Develop contextual ideas so that they blend usefully into the overall response.

Sample answer B

Holmes and Watson show their upper middle-class status when we see Holmes try to get information from Mrs Smith in this extract. Holmes flatters Mrs Smith's son to win her trust. In return, she gives him all of the information he needs. Mrs Smith immediately puts her trust in the gentleman detective, whereas she was suspicious of the 'monkey-faced chap' that Holmes is seeking – the escaped convict Jonathan Small. This implies that there was a strict social hierarchy at the time where everyone had their place.

AO3 An interesting supported observation which is linked to a thoughtful inference

Mrs Smith's class is shown through her mode of speech. The dialogue between Holmes and Mrs Smith is contrasting because Holmes is presented using standard English, representing the speech of the upper middle classes of the time, 'Dear little chap', whereas Mrs Smith and Jack are represented in dialect: 'I'd ha' thought nothin'', 'He tapped at the winder'.' Conan Doyle uses this technique elsewhere in the novel too, through the presentation of Mr Sherman. His dialect adds comedy to the episode with Watson, such as when he says, 'Don't mind that, sir: it's only a slow worm. It hain't got no fangs.'

AO2 Explores one of the writer's methods with effective evidence

AO1 Quotations are not smoothly embedded

The portrayals of these characters show the working class as people who are uneducated, easily tricked and who are quick to show respect to their 'betters'. 'Step in, sir', says Mr Sherman when he knows a friend of Holmes is calling. 'The Aurora, sir', says Mrs Smith in answer to Holmes's question. That same level of respect is not always returned or deserved as we can see in other parts of the novel.

AO1 A more thoughtful observation supported with some apt references

AO1 This point could be further developed

Before the boat chase on the Thames, Holmes refers to the workers leaving the yards as 'Dirty looking rascals' and patronises them due to their appearance, 'I suppose every one has some little immortal spark … You would not think it, to look at them.' This is the same attitude that leads to racist judgements being made about Tonga. Tonga has very little status in the novel, because he is a native of the Andaman Islands. Holmes's reference book describes the Islanders as 'naturally hideous' and 'a terror'. Holmes and Watson both refer to Tonga as 'a savage'. He is described as 'serving' Jonathan Small. Conan Doyle shows us that status at the time was unfair and always put the 'civilised' white man at the top.

AO2 A well-planned connection and link to wider exploration of the novel

AO3 A strong collection of textual evidence used to make a thoughtful point about social context

Jonathan Small, a white man, is also treated badly. Though Mrs Smith, in the extract, 'don't feel easy

AO3

An interesting contextual point, but it's not clear whether Conan Doyle himself is hypocritical or merely presents the hypocrisy in society

in my mind' about him, Small's story helps to show us how the British officers behaved towards him. Though both Major Sholto and Captain Morstan have military status, they behave in an immoral way, implying there was a great deal of hypocrisy in the social hierarchy of the time.

This hypocrisy also can be seen in the way Conan Doyle presents the status of women. Miss Morstan is a respectable middle-class woman, but without money or a profession of her own she relies on other people. Mrs Forrester points out to her that 'your fortune depends upon the issue of this search', which would provide her with an inheritance from her wayward father. This implies that within the upper and middle classes there were divisions of status based on gender as well as the divisions created by the class system.

AO1

Another interesting and thoughtful point though not supported with textual detail here

AO3

A useful idea which could have been more skilfully incorporated into the main essay and developed further

GOOD LEVEL

Comment:

This is a well-planned and organised response which explores a number of ideas in detail and shows a strong knowledge of the text. The text has been used thoughtfully to support ideas that are integrated into the interpretation. There is consideration of the writer's method and at times this is linked to context. This could have been developed further however, and a more conceptualised critical view taken.

For a High Level:

■ Explore the text with more of an overview.

■ Look at alternative interpretations or deeper meanings for some of the AO1 ideas.

■ Build AO2 and AO3 exploration more seamlessly into the response.

Sample answer C

"'The main thing with people of that sort," said Holmes, as we sat in the sheets of the wherry, "is never to let them think that their information can be of the slightest importance to you."' Though Holmes is undoubtedly using a technique by which to elicit information and move his case forward, the value judgements he makes here as a white upper middle class British man become immediately apparent. He makes a clear and divisive distinction between himself and Watson and the working-class woman with whom he is in conversation. These same disparaging attitudes are seen later in the novel when Holmes refers to the workers leaving the boatyard with the noun phrase 'Dirty looking rascals', the implication of which immediately sets up a connection between their position in life and their perceived respectability.

A01 — Ranges through the text skilfully to build an argument

A03 — A strong critical start, using the text judiciously and linking a contextual factor straight away

While Holmes takes a superior stance, Watson notes that the working-class individual has been reported as 'a soul concealed in an animal'. Similarly, the author of Holmes's reference book on the Andaman Islanders sets up a superior tone and relegates the native islanders to the status of beasts when they are described as 'naturally hideous' and 'fierce'. Indeed, this attitude is one that Holmes and Watson subscribe to themselves when they brand Tonga a 'savage' and shoot him in cold blood during the chase along the river. Watson's narrative uses language which relegates Tonga's status to that of less than human, describing him in abstract terms as being 'marked with all bestiality and cruelty'. Described as 'shrieking', 'gnashing' and 'menacing', Tonga is presented as a trapped, cornered wild animal, not a terrified man far away from home in fear for his life.

A02 — Close reading of language with precise references

This is in stark contrast to the way Tonga is described by Jonathan Small, as a companion who was 'stanch and true'. He was loyal to Small despite the fact he was stripped of equal status due to the colour of his skin and suffered the indignity of being exhibited 'at fairs and other such places as the black cannibal'.

A01 — More exploratory knowledge of the text shown with judicious references and well-embedded quotations

A01 — A further well-expressed and planned link

In the same way that Small commands Tonga's loyalty, Holmes commands the loyalty of other working-class characters throughout the novel. Somewhat ironically, given his attitudes and views, it is through the help and assistance of those characters that he is able to investigate more thoroughly. Without his acquaintance with McMurdo, for example, he would not gain entry to the murder scene at Pondicherry Lodge. He also makes use of the dog provided by Mr Sherman, and he employs the skills of the Baker Street Irregulars to make an initial search of the boatyards along the Thames. These characters automatically defer to Holmes and Watson, always using the mode of address 'Sir' in their dealings with them.

AO2 — Further consideration of method with judicious details

Conan Doyle presents these characters in a colourful and stereotypical way. He creates character through the use of their idiolect. This is often done for comic effect, for example when we hear Mr Sherman admonishing Watson as a 'drunken vagabone' or imagine the gossiping and superstitious tone of Mrs Smith who, 'don't feel easy in my mind' as she speculates on the shady character of Small.

Mrs Smith, however, places her immediate trust in the gentleman detective, she defers to him and shares both her concerns and the key information Holmes needs. His class and status carry with it a perception of respectability and trustworthiness.

AO3 — A conceptualised idea bringing together the whole essay conclusively, subtly linking context to meaning

This is more than ironic, however, when we consider the behaviour of other white British men with status in the novel. Captain Morstan and Major Sholto would be, on the surface, representatives of the British Empire and all of its values overseas. Their behaviours are far from respectable and their actions become criminal – though they are never brought to justice in the way that the working-class conscript Small is, or the brutal way that Tonga is punished for his complicity and loyalty.

AO2 — Well embedded quotation

Creating a mask of respectability, the upper middle classes show flawed values and judgements as fickle and unsubstantiated as those Mrs Smith has for the 'brown, monkey-faced chap' whom she is so inherently suspicious of.

VERY HIGH LEVEL

Comment:
This is a wide-ranging and conceptualised critical response. It shows a strong knowledge of the text and explores ideas by drawing on evidence, which is precise and judiciously chosen. Contextual points are subtly blended in to the points made for AO1 and AO2 rather than being dealt with in isolation. Expression is mature and convincing, leading to a well-structured argument.

Question 3

Read the following extract from Chapter 12 of *The Sign of the Four* (pages 111–12).

In this extract, Jonathan Small describes his experiences in Agra during the Indian Mutiny.

The whole country was up like a swarm of bees. Wherever the English could collect in little bands they held just the ground that their guns commanded. Everywhere else they were helpless fugitives. It was a fight of the millions against the hundreds;
5 and the cruellest part of it was that these men that we fought against, foot, horse, and gunners, were our own picked troops, whom we had taught and trained, handling our own weapons, and blowing our own bugle-calls. At Agra there were the 3d Bengal Fusiliers, some Sikhs, two troops of horse, and a battery
10 of artillery. A volunteer corps of clerks and merchants had been formed, and this I joined, wooden leg and all. We went out to meet the rebels at Shahgunge early in July, and we beat them back for a time, but our powder gave out, and we had to fall back upon the city. Nothing but the worst news came to us
15 from every side, – which is not to be wondered at, for if you look at the map you will see that we were right in the heart of it. Lucknow is rather better than a hundred miles to the east, and Cawnpore about as far to the south. From every point on the compass there was nothing but torture and murder and outrage.

20   The city of Agra is a great place, swarming with fanatics and fierce devil-worshippers of all sorts. Our handful of men were lost among the narrow, winding streets. Our leader moved across the river, therefore, and took up his position in the old fort at Agra. I don't know if any of you gentlemen have ever
25 read or heard anything of that old fort. It is a very queer place, – the queerest that ever I was in, and I have been in some rum corners, too. First of all, it is enormous in size. I should think that the enclosure must be acres and acres. There is a modern part, which took all our garrison, women, children, stores, and
30 everything else, with plenty of room over. But the modern part is nothing like the size of the old quarter, where nobody goes, and which is given over to the scorpions and centipedes.

'Conan Doyle presents India as a rebellious and brutal place.'

Starting with this extract, explore how far you agree with this opinion:

- in this extract
- in the novel as a whole.

[30 marks]

Annotated sample answers

Now, read the three sample answers that follow and, based on what you have read, try to allocate a level to your own work. Which of the three responses is your answer closest to? Don't be discouraged if your work doesn't seem as strong as some of the responses here – the point is to use these samples to learn about what is needed and then put it into practice in your own work. Conversely, you may have mentioned relevant ideas or points that don't appear in these responses; if this is the case, give yourself a pat on the back – it shows you are considering lots of good ideas.

Sample answer A

AO1
Makes a sensible start, but the quotation is not properly embedded and expression is a little informal

AO2
Touches on a method here but does not support or fully explain

The extract is taken from Jonathan Small's story of the Indian Mutiny against the British Army. Small describes the mutiny as massively brutal, 'There was nothing but torture and murder and outrage.'

Conan Doyle says how big the mutiny was with the phrase 'the millions against the hundreds' and this suggests India was a massive place with a very big population compared with the British. Small presents the British as the victims. It seems like Jonathan Small was only bothered about the safety of the British people hiding in the fort. He seems to be really honourable at first because he wants to be part of the force which protects 'all our garrison, women, children, stores, and everything else'.

Later in Small's story, Abdullah Khan says to Small, 'We only ask you to do that which your countrymen came to this land for', it suggests that the British have only been in India to get rich and that they have exploited the place and the people. Conan Doyle uses the Agra treasure as a symbol of this. The treasure had belonged to an Indian rajah but we find out later he was 'driven out' of his country. But, Thaddeus Sholto tells the others about his father and how he had lived in 'luxury' when he came home from India, even though we know he had not been an honourable man and had kept the stolen treasure for himself.

Jonathan Small thinks the treasure should be his and that he has a right to it even though it was stolen property and belonged in India, 'It is my treasure; and if I can't have the loot I'll take darned good care that no one else does.' This shows that the British had no respect at all for Indian culture or possessions and I think they didn't really understand the Indian people. In the extract, he describes Agra as 'swarming with fanatics and fierce devil-worshippers of all sorts.'

AO2
More ideas connected to meaning with some inference and support, showing knowledge of the novel, though this could be expressed more clearly with a more mature critical style

AO1
Avoid starting sentences with 'But'

AO3
Shows some understanding of an important contextual factor here

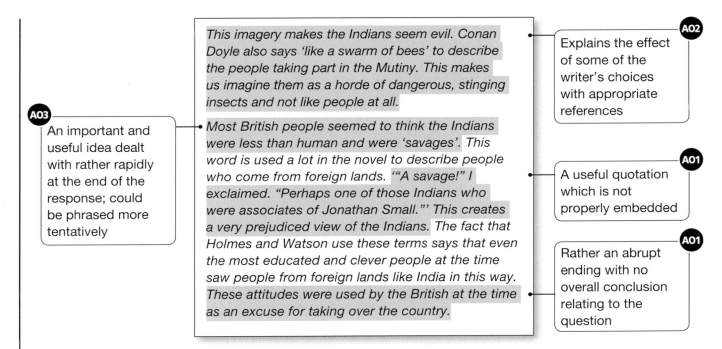

AO3

An important and useful idea dealt with rather rapidly at the end of the response; could be phrased more tentatively

This imagery makes the Indians seem evil. Conan Doyle also says 'like a swarm of bees' to describe the people taking part in the Mutiny. This makes us imagine them as a horde of dangerous, stinging insects and not like people at all.

Most British people seemed to think the Indians were less than human and were 'savages'. This word is used a lot in the novel to describe people who come from foreign lands. '"A savage!" I exclaimed. "Perhaps one of those Indians who were associates of Jonathan Small."' This creates a very prejudiced view of the Indians. The fact that Holmes and Watson use these terms says that even the most educated and clever people at the time saw people from foreign lands like India in this way. These attitudes were used by the British at the time as an excuse for taking over the country.

AO2

Explains the effect of some of the writer's choices with appropriate references

AO1

A useful quotation which is not properly embedded

AO1

Rather an abrupt ending with no overall conclusion relating to the question

MID LEVEL

Comment:
There is clear explanation in this response that shows some understanding of the key issues. There are a number of relevant references and quotations used in support. Some of the methods used by the writer have been identified though the effects of these are not always fully explained. The answer would benefit from more formal expression and a conclusion that directly answers the question.

For a Good Level:

- Use references more effectively to justify the explanations given.
- Identify and explore the effects of a greater range of methods.
- Ensure that contextual factors are more thoroughly explained.

Sample answer B

AO2

Identifies Conan Doyle's method, though the effect here could be explored in detail

Conan Doyle presents the Indian Mutiny against the British through a story within the story. It is told from Small's point of view and he presents it as a bloody and brutal attack on the British forces and plantation owners by the Indian sepoys.

In the extract, the attack is described as 'a fight of the millions against the hundreds', showing the British were hugely outnumbered, yet they are presented in a patriotic way by Small. He reports that, 'Wherever the English could collect in little bands they held just the ground that their guns commanded.' This implies that the English were brave, but it also suggests the vast numbers of people who had been controlled and exploited through British rule. We might infer that this would eventually cause frustrations among the Indian population, leading to rebellion.

AO1

Makes a thoughtful inference in response to the task

AO1

Another considered inference which uses the text as support

Small seems shocked and outraged by the actions of the Indians, yet takes part in brutal acts himself against Achmet the merchant and the convict guard on the Andaman Islands. He kills the guard when he 'knocked the whole front of his skull in'. Conan Doyle exposes the hypocrisy of colonisation when we see how Small respects and values the lives of the white British sheltering in the fort, but does not seem to care about Achmet as 'the thought of his treasure turned me hard and bitter.'

Conan Doyle gives us more insight into the appalling behaviour and hypocrisy of some of the British officers through the actions of Captain Morstan and Major Sholto. They become motivated by greed and seem to appear as a symbol of why the British were in India in the first place. This is summarised for us later through the words of Abdullah Khan – one of the Four – who says to Small, 'We only ask you to do that which your countrymen came to this land for. We ask you to be rich'.

AO1

Supports a thoughtful idea with a key quotation but could be further developed

AO3

Makes use of contextual knowledge, though not linked seamlessly

India is presented as a land of possibility for all classes of white men. Small used India as a means of escape from his village life, some owned plantations and others had a career in the military. We know that Major Sholto came back from the colony and, despite his shameful behaviour, 'lived in great luxury'. However, we are aware as readers that much of this wealth was stolen property. His only regret on his deathbed was his 'treatment of poor Morstan's orphan'. He does not seem to regret his dishonourable actions in India or his theft of the treasure.

AO1

Shows some well-supported knowledge of the wider text

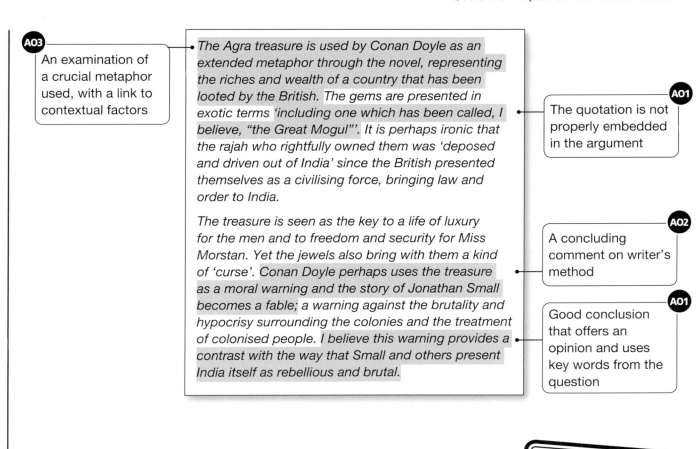

AO3
An examination of a crucial metaphor used, with a link to contextual factors

The Agra treasure is used by Conan Doyle as an extended metaphor through the novel, representing the riches and wealth of a country that has been looted by the British. The gems are presented in exotic terms 'including one which has been called, I believe, "the Great Mogul"'. It is perhaps ironic that the rajah who rightfully owned them was 'deposed and driven out of India' since the British presented themselves as a civilising force, bringing law and order to India.

The treasure is seen as the key to a life of luxury for the men and to freedom and security for Miss Morstan. Yet the jewels also bring with them a kind of 'curse'. Conan Doyle perhaps uses the treasure as a moral warning and the story of Jonathan Small becomes a fable; a warning against the brutality and hypocrisy surrounding the colonies and the treatment of colonised people. I believe this warning provides a contrast with the way that Small and others present India itself as rebellious and brutal.

AO1
The quotation is not properly embedded in the argument

AO2
A concluding comment on writer's method

AO1
Good conclusion that offers an opinion and uses key words from the question

GOOD LEVEL

Comment:
This response shows a detailed knowledge of the text and ideas are organised methodically and well supported. There is some strong contextual knowledge, though at times this appears to be the starting point for ideas rather than being seamlessly linked to them. The response explores a number of methods, though again these could be better developed.

For a High Level:

- Work on a more sophisticated style to blend ideas seamlessly together.
- Ensure all contextual points are drawn out of the analysis rather than being the starting point for ideas.
- Explore methods in a more wide-ranging way with more effective use of textual details.

Sample answer C

AO1 Strong personal response

I believe that this extract from 'The Sign of the Four' should be viewed in the context of Conan Doyle's central metaphor. Representing everything the British saw as exotic, alluring and ripe for exploiting, the Agra treasure stands as a symbol of India itself. Described in lavish terms as 'diamonds of the first water … ninety-seven very fine emeralds', the treasure is a bittersweet symbol and a 'cursed' reminder of the price to be paid for the brutal exploitation of other lands and peoples.

AO2 An initial exploration of the writer's method linked seamlessly to a contextual idea

AO1 Links the extract skilfully to an idea from earlier in the novel with a precise reference to support

It is Abdullah Khan who gives a stark and honest reminder of why the British were in India when he requests of Small: 'We only ask you to do that which your countrymen came to this land for. We ask you to be rich'. This is borne out by the fact that Major Sholto, again representing the British Officer class whose fortunes were made in colonised lands, 'prospered in India'. He has lived out his life 'in great luxury', though is also shrouded in guilt and fear as a result of his greed and hypocrisy.

Captain Morstan shared this hypocrisy and yet both Sholto's sons and Morstan's daughter are seen as the heirs to the treasure. There is little concern that this is stolen property, plundered from India, from a dispossessed and deposed rajah, with innocent lives lost in the process. This sense of entitlement is vividly depicted in the extract where Small laments the 'cruellest part of it' – the fact that the Indians turned their British-suppled weapons on their masters, showing that he has complete disregard for the colonised people. This lack of concern is shared not only by the Sholtos and Small, but also by Watson who unquestioningly assumes 'part of it, belonged rightfully to Miss Morstan'. Mrs Forrester sees the treasure as a way for Mary to secure her future, with no regard for its provenance, and, indeed, relegates those whose lives have been destroyed to characters in a story, '"It is a romance!" cried Mrs Forrester.'

AO2 Sensitive response to a key quotation, with a clear and strong effect highlighted

AO1 Convincing critical analysis with judicious choices to support

AO3 A clear and well-supported idea preceded by a strong overview sentence

India is portrayed as a land of opportunity, with riches to be greedily exploited by the colonising nation. However, within the extract, it is also seen as a place that is dangerous, wild and to be feared; a place 'swarming with fanatics and fierce devil-worshippers'. The native peoples far outnumber the colonisers; learning as we do that the mutiny was a 'fight of the millions against the hundreds'. In order to justify the brutal oppression of the masses, those masses had to be seen as inferior, less than human and 'savage'.

A03

A convincing analysis linking contextual ideas seamlessly with inferences, all supported with textual references from throughout the text

A01

Develops the idea concisely with further well-chosen textual detail

A01

Strong personal interpretation to close

This is shown through Small's eyes through the portrayal of the sepoys as 'a swarm of bees' and individually by Conan Doyle through the description of Tonga. His use of the blowpipe is seen as a result of his 'natural instincts for savagery'.

By contrast, the English woman and her home may be seen as the absolute antithesis to the 'savagery' of the colonies and representative of all that was civilised and harmonious. Conan Doyle paints a picture of this through the eyes of Dr Watson when he describes Mrs Forrester's home as a sanctuary from the 'wild dark business' of the case. This suggests the English home was the place a man could return to following his own 'wild, dark business' in uncivilised and dangerous colonies overseas, peopled by 'savages'. This romanticised view of the conquering British hero is further emphasised by Mary's description of Holmes and Watson as 'two knight-errants'.

Mary Morstan does, however, act as a moral yardstick against this hypocritical and highly prejudiced backdrop. The fact she has no desire for the treasure and does not anticipate its arrival with greed sets her apart from the four thieves, her own father and Major Sholto. Mary, is, however, rooted in British values and culture. Crucially, she has not been subject to what many readers at the time would have seen as the uncivilised influence of British India. I would argue that Conan Doyle seemingly uses this influence to exonerate the brutal behaviours and actions of the British military officers whose shameful behaviour was the catalyst for the 'wild dark business' of the rebellion and the case itself.

A02

Close conceptualised analysis of writer's method with well-embedded quotation

A03

A further more subtle contextual point

VERY HIGH LEVEL

Comment:

A skilful answer showing a wide variety of knowledge and making secure critical points. Ideas are supported with well-judged references. Ideas regarding context and method are skilfully interwoven. This helps to create a highly conceptualised piece overall with written flair and a convincing argument.

Question 4

Read the following extract from Chapter 3 of *The Sign of the Four* (pages 19–20).

In this extract, Holmes, Watson and Miss Morstan travel to the Lyceum Theatre to meet an unknown person.

It was a September evening, and not yet seven o'clock, but the day had been a dreary one, and a dense drizzly fog lay low upon the great city. Mud-colored clouds drooped sadly over the muddy streets. Down the Strand the lamps were but misty splotches of
5   diffused light which threw a feeble circular glimmer upon the slimy pavement. The yellow glare from the shop-windows streamed out into the steamy, vaporous air, and threw a murky, shifting radiance across the crowded thoroughfare. There was, to my mind, something eerie and ghost-like in the endless procession
10   of faces which flitted across these narrow bars of light,–sad faces and glad, haggard and merry. Like all human kind, they flitted from the gloom into the light, and so back into the gloom once more. I am not subject to impressions, but the dull, heavy evening, with the strange business upon which we were engaged, combined to
15   make me nervous and depressed. I could see from Miss Morstan's manner that she was suffering from the same feeling. Holmes alone could rise superior to petty influences. He held his open note-book upon his knee, and from time to time he jotted down figures and memoranda in the light of his pocket-lantern.

20   At the Lyceum Theatre the crowds were already thick at the side-entrances. In front a continuous stream of hansoms and four-wheelers were rattling up, discharging their cargoes of shirt-fronted men and beshawled, bediamonded women. We had hardly reached the third pillar, which was our rendezvous, before a small,
25   dark, brisk man in the dress of a coachman accosted us.

'Are you the parties who come with Miss Morstan?' he asked.

'I am Miss Morstan, and these two gentlemen are my friends,' said she.

He bent a pair of wonderfully penetrating and questioning
30   eyes upon us. 'You will excuse me, miss,' he said with a certain dogged manner, 'but I was to ask you to give me your word that neither of your companions is a police-officer.'

'I give you my word on that,' she answered.

Starting with this extract, how does Conan Doyle use London as a setting?

Write about:

■ how Conan Doyle uses London in this extract
■ how Conan Doyle uses London in the novel as a whole.

[30 marks]

Annotated sample answers

Now, read the three sample answers that follow and, based on what you have read, try to allocate a level to your own work. Which of the three responses is your answer closest to? Don't be discouraged if your work doesn't seem as strong as some of the responses here – the point is to use these samples to learn about what is needed and then put it into practice in your own work. Conversely, you may have mentioned relevant ideas or points that don't appear in these responses; if this is the case, give yourself a pat on the back – it shows you are considering lots of good ideas.

Sample answer A

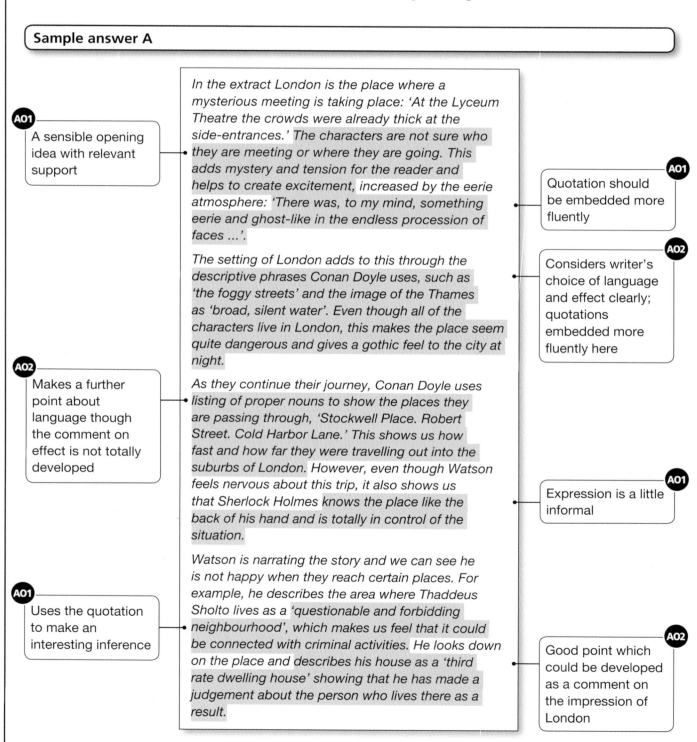

AO1
A sensible opening idea with relevant support

In the extract London is the place where a mysterious meeting is taking place: 'At the Lyceum Theatre the crowds were already thick at the side-entrances.' The characters are not sure who they are meeting or where they are going. This adds mystery and tension for the reader and helps to create excitement, increased by the eerie atmosphere: 'There was, to my mind, something eerie and ghost-like in the endless procession of faces ...'.

AO1
Quotation should be embedded more fluently

The setting of London adds to this through the descriptive phrases Conan Doyle uses, such as 'the foggy streets' and the image of the Thames as 'broad, silent water'. Even though all of the characters live in London, this makes the place seem quite dangerous and gives a gothic feel to the city at night.

AO2
Considers writer's choice of language and effect clearly; quotations embedded more fluently here

AO2
Makes a further point about language though the comment on effect is not totally developed

As they continue their journey, Conan Doyle uses listing of proper nouns to show the places they are passing through, 'Stockwell Place. Robert Street. Cold Harbor Lane.' This shows us how fast and how far they were travelling out into the suburbs of London. However, even though Watson feels nervous about this trip, it also shows us that Sherlock Holmes knows the place like the back of his hand and is totally in control of the situation.

AO1
Expression is a little informal

AO1
Uses the quotation to make an interesting inference

Watson is narrating the story and we can see he is not happy when they reach certain places. For example, he describes the area where Thaddeus Sholto lives as a 'questionable and forbidding neighbourhood', which makes us feel that it could be connected with criminal activities. He looks down on the place and describes his house as a 'third rate dwelling house' showing that he has made a judgement about the person who lives there as a result.

AO2
Good point which could be developed as a comment on the impression of London

AO1

A useful link to another part of the novel with an interesting inference

AO2

Mentions a language technique with example

He also has this impression when he visits Mr Sherman's shop. It is described as 'shabby' and in 'the lower quarter of Lambeth'. However, it helps the reader to see London is a very varied place and is a home to many interesting characters.

Conan Doyle shows different sides to London as he contrasts the description of the shop with Mrs Forrester's house. He describes this house in a very beautiful way as a 'tranquil English home'. He uses lots of different places in London to show how different classes of people all lived side by side in one place that was growing bigger. We see this when he describes London as having, 'monster tentacles which the giant city was throwing out into the country.'

London is used again when Watson and Holmes take Toby for a 'six-mile trudge' to follow the trail left by the creosote. Listing is used to show all of the places they walk through on their search: 'Streatham, Brixton, Camberwell'. This journey through London means that Watson and Holmes have time to talk through the whole case and the clues and they share all of this with the reader. It also leads to Mordecai Smith's boatyard and the river.

The river Thames is used for the final chase where Jonathan Small is caught. This is the climax of the story. Here the river is used to make the chase more exciting and the boat chase creates speed and drama. Interesting verbs are used to bring the chase to life, such as 'We flashed past barges', 'We shot through the Pool.' The Thames is also the place where Jonathan Small throws away the treasure so that no one else can have it.

Overall, Conan Doyle uses London to add mystery, excitement and tension to the novel but also to take the reader on all of the journeys in the novel with the characters.

AO3

Aims to consider context using the quotation to trigger the idea, but not analysed or developed

AO2

Language features identified but examples unrelated to the question

MID LEVEL

Comment:
Though a little informal at times, this has some clear ideas, which have been supported with relevant quotations. Inferences made are well explained in the main. Some interesting ideas about context are included though not always developed. Analysis of methods tends to focus on language features and, again, effects are not always developed

For a Good Level:

- Plan more of an overview to avoid moving chronologically through the text.
- Explore other aspects of the writer's method as well as language features.
- Blend contextual ideas more skilfully.

Sample answer B

 AO1

Appropriate use of quotation in opening sentence

AO2

A well chosen point made on the use of a language technique, but language could be explored further

AO2

Solid interpretation of language choice

AO1

A confident idea with apt references; thoughtful inference

London is presented by Conan Doyle as a sprawling metropolis with its 'monster tentacles … throwing out into the country.' In this way, it mirrors the story itself and the way the story unfolds into 'unknown places'. In the extract, Conan Doyle takes all the main characters away from the comfort and safety of Baker Street and despite the fact they are in 'a crowded thoroughfare', Watson tells us of his 'nervous and depressed' feelings. The idea of a mysterious meeting, with the instruction not to bring the police, sets the reader up for rising tension in the story. This is emphasised through the use of personification. The evening itself is described as dreary, with 'mud-colored clouds' that 'drooped sadly'. Conan Doyle stereotypes London as a scene of gothic horror, with 'a murky, shifting radiance' and 'a dense drizzly fog' such as readers might associate with its past and infamous murderers like Jack the Ripper.

The gothic foreboding and sense of threat is further heightened with the description of the 'ghost-like … procession of faces which flitted'. The inhabitants of London seem like ghosts as they move around the city. This otherworldliness suggests that the characters are going into the unknown and shows that the outcome is uncertain and mysterious.

Despite the fact the journey takes them to a 'questionable and forbidding' part of London, neighbourhood', it seems that only Watson is anxious and fearful. Miss Morstan is described as 'resolute and collected' and Holmes as 'never at fault'. Holmes seems to mentally map their mystery journey as they travel through the streets, saying 'Rochester Row, … Now Vincent Square… .' This shows us how familiar he is with the streets of London and his knowledge of the place itself seems to reflect how Holmes is always in control.

This sense of control is further highlighted when Holmes and Watson embark on a 'six mile trudge' through the streets with Toby the bloodhound. This journey takes us through London at night and potentially symbolises the way that Holmes's mind works. Alongside this, as Holmes and Watson walk through 'Streatham, Brixton, Camberwell …', Holmes's mind is working at top speed. He pieces together the evidence so far until Watson, 'could see by the gleam in Holmes's eyes that he thought we were nearing the end of our journey'.

The River Thames is the scene of the climax of the novel and again represents a crazed journey at top speed. This time the speed of the journey adds drama,

AO1

Solid supported textual knowledge shown with some appreciation of writer's methods

AO3

Useful reference to social context linked to depiction of setting

AO1

Apt quotation, fluently embedded

AO1

Another detailed and thoughtful example of inferential reading; well supported with embedded quotation

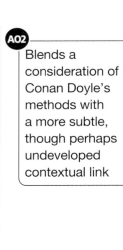

AO2 Blends a consideration of Conan Doyle's methods with a more subtle, though perhaps undeveloped contextual link

anxiety and heightened tension. *The metaphor of a hunt is used to show this when Watson comments, 'never did sport give me such a wild thrill as this mad, flying man-hunt down the Thames'. Conan Doyle lists all of the types of boats they fly past on the river as their 'powerful engines whizzed and clanked'. We are reminded of the industrial nature of London and the links to other countries as they speed past 'West India Docks'.*

London is also used to represent people and social class. How Conan Doyle presents different places in London helps to show the social attitudes of the time. Watson describes Sholto's neighbourhood as 'questionable and forbidding'. Contrastingly, he presents Mrs Forrester's house as a 'tranquil English home' not near any 'tawdry brilliance of public houses'. It seems that Conan Doyle uses different locations to make us as readers make judgements about them and the people that live there.

AO3 A final contextual point to build the conclusion

AO1 A rather weak final sentence; could be stronger and more precise

Comment:
This is a detailed and thoughtful response, which covers a lot of ground. There is some secure knowledge of the text and some thoughtful and insightful inferences are made. The response aims to blend contextual ideas though the conclusion could be developed further and methods explored more fully. There are brief references to the play's context which could be more integrated into the argument.

For a High Level:

- Create more balance in the response between meanings and methods.
- Work on a more concise, conceptualised overview.
- Create a more effective conclusion.

Sample answer C

London – the capital city and the very heart of the British Empire – is used by Conan Doyle in this novel both as setting and symbol. It is the territory of Sherlock Holmes whose intimate knowledge of its highways and people show him to be in control, even when other protagonists lead him on journeys of mystery and danger.

AO2 — A strong, confident opening overview statement from which to draw out the response

AO3 — Securely links a point about methods with a contextual inference

In the extract, Conan Doyle creates a contrasting image of 'shirt-fronted men' and 'bediamonded women' with the gothic description of the evening where a 'dense drizzly fog lay low upon the great city.' It seems as though London, despite its glamorous façade, has a 'murky, shifting' underbelly, which we see resonate through the novel as a whole. Sherlock's mind computes and maps the journey away from the glamour and dazzling lights of London's theatre district and is 'never at fault' as they enter the murk and gloom of its 'labyrinth of streets' and darkened suburbs.

AO2 — Crisply expressed ideas with embedded textual detail

AO1 — Shows a strong and wide-ranging textual knowledge

London is shown to be a city of contrasts but one with which Holmes is totally familiar. His network of potentially dubious contacts is revealed to us time and again as we move from Pondicherry Lodge, to Sherman's shop to the eyes and ears of the Baker Street Irregulars along the riverbank. Conan Doyle presents the working-class characters in the novel as a source of information and help. However, our perceptions of them are coloured by the descriptions of their place in London, such as Sherman's shop located in 'a row of shabby two-storied brick houses in the lower quarters of Lambeth'.

AO1 — Well embedded quotations

Watson is disturbed by the 'questionable and forbidding neighbourhood' in which Sholto lives. He exhibits distaste at his 'third rate dwelling house', suggesting the suburbs themselves, spreading their 'monster tentacles ... out into the country', could be analogous to something fearful and malevolent. This is in contrast to the 'tranquil English home' where Mrs Forrester and Miss Morstan await news of their 'two knight-errants'. Here, respectability, morality and all of the surface values of the British Empire are encapsulated in the 'hall light shining through stained glass, the barometer and the bright stair-rods'.

AO3 — A subtle textual detail used to make a perceptive contextual point

AO1 — Again, a subtle textual reference is used to make a perceptive point with skilfully woven contextual links

These references are echoed when the River Thames becomes a symbol, not only for the pursuit of justice, but also of Empire. Given almost religious significance, Watson reports that, 'as we passed the City the last rays of the sun were gilding the cross upon the summit of St. Paul's'.

AO3

A further perceptive detail of context

AO2

Develops the point to explore language and method with judicious references

AO1

Skilfully uses the text to bring together a confident and critically mature conclusion

This beautiful and iconic image contrasts with the 'thrill' of the 'mad, flying man-hunt down the Thames'. Conan Doyle uses barbaric imagery to describe the way that Small and Tonga, 'our quarry', were hunted down once they were beyond the reaches of the 'West India Docks'.

The boats and shipyards along the Thames serve to remind us of the importance of London as heart of empire and the dark brutality which accompanied those journeys is exemplified through the story of Jonathan Small. In the 'wild and desolate place' beyond the reach of the 'melancholy Plumstead Marshes' both the Agra treasure and Tonga, the 'savage, distorted creature', are consigned to and swallowed up by the 'dark ooze at the bottom of the Thames'. This symbolises how far London's 'monster tentacles' have reached as the heart of the British Empire.

VERY HIGH LEVEL

Comment:

A skilful and mature response which weaves together all of the assessment objectives, particularly through its confident opening and conclusion. This response uses original textual references to build a highly convincing argument with a strong and mature critical style.

PART THREE: FURTHER YORK NOTES PRACTICE TESTS WITH SHORT ANSWERS

Here are three further questions on the text in a similar style to the ones you might face in your exam. Taking into account what you have learnt from the mark schemes on pages 7–8, and the sample responses to the other questions, use Questions 5 to 7 as you wish. You may choose to:

■ plan ideas

■ write opening paragraphs or part answers

■ write full answers at your own speed

■ write full answers to a set time limit.

Once you have finished, you can check to see if you have covered some of the key points suggested in the Answers section, and make a judgement about what level you have achieved.

Question 5

Read the following extract from Chapter 6 of *The Sign of the Four* (pages 49–50).

In this extract, Athelney Jones arrests Thaddeus Sholto at the crime scene at Pondicherry Lodge.

'… How does all that fit into your theory?'

'Confirms it in every respect,' said the fat detective, pompously. 'House full of Indian curiosities. Thaddeus brought this up, and if this splinter be poisonous Thaddeus may as well have made murderous use of it as any other man. The card is some hocus-pocus,
5   – a blind, as like as not. The only question is, how did he depart? Ah, of course, here is a hole in the roof.' With great activity, considering his bulk, he sprang up the steps and squeezed through into the garret, and immediately afterwards we heard his exulting voice proclaiming that he had found the trap-door.

'He can find something,' remarked Holmes, shrugging his shoulders. 'He has occasional
10   glimmerings of reason. *Il n'y a pas des sots si incommodes que ceux qui on de l'esprit!*'

'You see!' said Athelney Jones, reappearing down the steps again. 'Facts are better than mere theories, after all. My view of the case is confirmed. There is a trap-door communicating with the roof, and it is partly open.'

'It was I who opened it.'

15   'Oh, indeed! You did notice it, then?' He seemed a little crestfallen at the discovery. 'Well, whoever noticed it, it shows how our gentleman got away. Inspector!'

'Yes, sir,' from the passage.

'Ask Mr. Sholto to step this way. – Mr. Sholto, it is my duty to inform you that anything which you may say will be used against you. I arrest you in the queen's name as being
20   concerned in the death of your brother.'

'There, now! Didn't I tell you!' cried the poor little man, throwing out his hands, and looking from one to the other of us.

'Don't trouble yourself about it, Mr. Sholto,' said Holmes. 'I think that I can engage to clear you of the charge.'

25   'Don't promise too much, Mr. Theorist, – don't promise too much!' snapped the detective. 'You may find it a harder matter than you think.'

Starting with this extract, how does Conan Doyle present the character of Athelney Jones?

Write about:

■ how Conan Doyle presents the character of Athelney Jones in this extract
■ how Conan Doyle presents the character of Athelney Jones in the novel as a whole.

[30 marks]

Question 6

Read the following extract from Chapter 4 of *The Sign of the Four* (page 28).

In this extract, Thaddeus Sholto recounts how his father shared a secret with his sons on his deathbed.

'I have only one thing,' he said, 'which weighs upon my mind at this supreme moment. It is my treatment of poor Morstan's orphan. The cursed greed which has been my besetting sin through life has withheld from her the treasure, half at least of

5   which should have been hers. And yet I have made no use of it myself, – so blind and foolish a thing is avarice. The mere feeling of possession has been so dear to me that I could not bear to share it with another. See that chaplet dipped with pearls beside the quinine-bottle. Even that I could not bear to part with,

10   although I had got it out with the design of sending it to her. You, my sons, will give her a fair share of the Agra treasure. But send her nothing – not even the chaplet – until I am gone. After all, men have been as bad as this and have recovered.

'I will tell you how Morstan died,' he continued. 'He had

15   suffered for years from a weak heart, but he concealed it from every one. I alone knew it. When in India, he and I, through a remarkable chain of circumstances, came into possession of a considerable treasure. I brought it over to England, and on the night of Morstan's arrival he came straight over here to claim

20   his share. He walked over from the station, and was admitted by my faithful Lal Chowdar, who is now dead. Morstan and I had a difference of opinion as to the division of the treasure, and we came to heated words. Morstan had sprung out of his chair in a paroxysm of anger, when he suddenly pressed

25   his hand to his side, his face turned a dusky hue, and he fell backwards, cutting his head against the corner of the treasure-chest. When I stooped over him I found, to my horror, that he was dead.'

Starting with this extract, how does Conan Doyle present different attitudes to wealth?

Write about:

■ how Conan Doyle presents different attitudes to wealth in this extract
■ how Conan Doyle presents different attitudes to wealth in the novel as a whole.

[30 marks]

Question 7

Read the following extract from Chapter 5 of *The Sign of the Four* (page 36).

In this extract, Holmes and Watson arrive at Pondicherry Lodge with Miss Morstan and Thaddeus Sholto.

Inside, a gravel path wound through desolate grounds to a huge clump of a house, square and prosaic, all plunged in shadow save where a moonbeam struck one corner and glimmered in a garret window. The vast size of the building, with its gloom and its deathly silence, struck a chill to the heart. Even Thaddeus Sholto seemed ill at ease, and
5   the lantern quivered and rattled in his hand.

'I cannot understand it,' he said. 'There must be some mistake. I distinctly told Bartholomew that we should be here, and yet there is no light in his window. I do not know what to make of it.'

'Does he always guard the premises in this way?' asked Holmes.

10   'Yes; he has followed my father's custom. He was the favorite son, you know, and I sometimes think that my father may have told him more than he ever told me. That is Bartholomew's window up there where the moonshine strikes. It is quite bright, but there is no light from within, I think.'

'None,' said Holmes. 'But I see the glint of a light in that little window beside the door.'

15   'Ah, that is the housekeeper's room. That is where old Mrs. Bernstone sits. She can tell us all about it. But perhaps you would not mind waiting here for a minute or two, for if we all go in together and she has no word of our coming she may be alarmed. But hush! What is that?'

He held up the lantern, and his hand shook until the circles of light flickered and waved
20   all round us. Miss Morstan seized my wrist, and we all stood with thumping hearts, straining our ears. From the great black house there sounded through the silent night the saddest and most pitiful of sounds, – the shrill, broken whimpering of a frightened woman.

'It is Mrs. Bernstone,' said Sholto. 'She is the only woman in the house.'

Starting with this extract, how does Conan Doyle use the setting of Pondicherry Lodge as a way of adding mystery and tension?

Write about:

■ how Conan Doyle uses the setting of Pondicherry Lodge as a way of adding mystery and tension in the extract

■ how Conan Doyle uses the setting of Pondicherry Lodge as a way of adding mystery and tension in the novel as a whole.

[30 marks]

ANSWERS

Short (indicative content) answers are given for Questions 5 to 7 below and on the following pages, covering the three main Assessment Objectives.

Question 5

Your answer could include the following:

AO1

- In the extract Jones is presented as loud and pompous.
- Also within the extract Jones is sceptical and suspicious of Holmes's methods and feels his work is based on theory and not police experience.
- Elsewhere in the novel, he shows a less pompous side when he asks for help from Holmes when his own enquiry draws a blank.
- At the end of the novel, he reverts back to his superior manner once Small has been safely caught and brought to justice.

AO2

- The writer uses irony in the extract when Jones jumps to conclusions about the case and this creates humour.
- Jones's short exclamatory sentences help to create the impression of him making snap judgements in contrast to Holmes's methodical approach.
- Later in the novel, there is use of hyperbole in the newspaper account that presents Jones as having almost solved the case single-handedly.
- Once Small has been captured Jones switches to using the inclusive pronoun 'we' to share in the success.

AO3

- Within the extract Jones appears as one of the conventions of the classic detective story where official police officers provide contrast to the unique abilities of the detective.
- Sherlock Holmes's approach compared with Jones's links to the origins of the use of forensics in detective work.
- Jones is representative of the systems of justice at the time and he helps to show the flaws in that system through the mistakes he makes.

Question 6

Your answer could include the following:

AO1

- The extract gives the first mention of the Agra treasure and Sholto shows his guilt for withholding it from Mary Morstan through his own greed.
- The extract shows how Captain Morstan is connected to the treasure and that others are also seeking it.
- Elsewhere in the novel, we learn how Small was encouraged to gain wealth through being an accomplice in murder as part of 'the Four'.
- Later, we are given more insight into the greed and desperation of Morstan and Sholto in particular, who had gambling debts.
- Watson has concerns that increased wealth will mean Mary would not be interested in him as a marriage partner. Later in the novel, we find out that Mary was not interested in the huge wealth this would bring, despite the change it would bring to her status.

AO2

- In the extract Conan Doyle uses language filled with abstract nouns such as 'greed' and 'avarice' to show the negative impact of the huge wealth on those connected with it.
- Conan Doyle uses the technique of the story within the story to present Major Sholto's perspective through Thaddeus.
- Elsewhere in the novel, Conan Doyle uses the treasure symbolically to represent wealth; but also wealth that has been looted from India.
- On more than one occasion the word 'curse' or 'cursed' is used by characters to describe the treasure; perhaps highlighting the many immoral attitudes to gaining wealth.

AO3

- In the extract the use of Major Sholto and Captain Morstan helps us to understand how those in positions of military authority behaved dishonourably whilst representing their country.
- Throughout the novel, the Agra treasure is linked with the exploitation of India through greed and the desire to acquire wealth.
- Different moral attitudes are displayed through the novel by different characters in terms of their attitude to wealth: Mary Morstan is seen as the moral yardstick compared with many of the male characters, including her own father, Major Sholto and 'the Four'.

Question 7

Your answer could include the following:

AO1

- The house is a locked and forbidding place, which has a sinister air.
- The house is discovered to be a crime scene where Bartholomew Sholto is found murdered in his mysterious laboratory.
- Later in the novel, Holmes explores this crime scene forensically and we see how his methods of investigation compare with those of Jones.
- The house becomes linked to all aspects of the mystery such as the death of Captain Morstan and Major Sholto and the hiding place of the stolen treasure.

AO2

- Conan Doyle makes use of gothic conventions to describe the house and its grounds to create mystery and tension both through the language choices and the use of pathetic fallacy.
- The use of the locked door later in the chapter is symbolic of the isolation and fear caused by hoarding the treasure.
- Conan Doyle introduces the idea of duality to show the opposing characters of the twins and the balance between good and evil in the novel as a whole.

AO3

- The extract raises issues of gender when the women are portrayed as weak and fearful and are later marginalised and excluded from the main action and its 'horrors'.
- The extract uses some of the stereotypical features of the horror story, with references to fear, darkness, moonlight and the piercing scream.
- The later discovery of the laboratory at Pondicherry Lodge reveals details about the Victorian desire to acquire scientific knowledge, exemplified by Holmes's forensic search.
- The later discovery of the thorn at Pondicherry Lodge raises issues about the foreign influence on the plot, including the fact that the treasure comes from colonial India.